8-Stage Learning Design Framework: Using Student Profiles and Personas

An introduction to the 8-SLDF, and the first stage, that of creating and using student profiles and personas to ensure effective course and programme design

Dr Simon Paul Atkinson is a New Zealand based educator with over 25 years' experience of academic and faculty development practice.

First published 2024

By Sijen Education

43 Pembroke Road, Northland, Wellington, 6012, New Zealand (sijen.com).

© 2024 Simon Paul Atkinson

All rights reserved. No part of this book may be reprinted or reproduced or utilised in any form or buy any electronic, mechanical, or other means, now known or hereafter invented, including photocopying and recording, or in any information storage or retrieval system, without permission in writing from the publishers.

Trademark notice: product or corporate names may be trademarks or registered trademarks and are used only for identification and explanation without intent to infringe.

Cover image created by the author

8-Stage Learning Design Framework: Using Student Profiles and Personas

ISBN: 978-0-473-70414-8 (pbk)
ISBN: 978-0-473-70415-5 (Kindle)
ISBN: 978-0-473-70416-2 (PDF)
ISBN: 978-0-473-70417-9 (Apple Books)
ISBN: 978-0-473-70418-6 (Audio Book)

Typeface is Calibri

For Jeanette.

Contents

LIST OF FIGURES 1
LIST OF TABLES 1
AUTHOR BIOGRAPHY 2
PREFACE 3
ACKNOWLEDGEMENTS 4
STRUCTURE OF THIS BOOK 5

THE CHALLENGE OF COURSE DESIGN 8

Activity 1: Future Learning 12

DESIGN APPROACHES: FRAMEWORKS, PATTERNS, MODELS AND PHILOSOPHIES 13

ADDIE 15
Merrill's Principles of Instruction (MPI) 17
Gagné's Nine Steps for Instruction 19
Universal Design for Learning - UDL 21
Bloom's (Cognitive) Taxonomy 23
Other Approaches 26
SOLE (Student Owned Learning Engagement) model 27
DIAL-e (Digital Artifacts for Learner Engagement) Framework 29
ABC Learning Design 31
7C's 32
Activity 2: Design Approaches 34

8-STAGE LEARNING DESIGN FRAMEWORK 35

VERY BRIEF HISTORY 36
SUMMARY OF THE EIGHT STAGES 37
Overview – Learning Philosophy 37
Stage 1: Designing for Students: Personas and Profiles 39
Stage 2: Designing for Professional or Discipline Contexts 39

Stage 3: Media Choices Informing Design................ 39
  Stage 4: Writing Good Learning Outcomes and
  Objectives.. 40
  Stage 5: Developing a Meaningful Assessment Strategy
  40
  Stage 6: Designing Engaging Learning Opportunities 41
  Stage 7: Creating Opportunities for Feedback
  Throughout 41
  Stage 8: In-course and Post Course Evaluation
  Strategies 42

STAGE 1: STUDENT PROFILES OR PERSONAS 44

  STUDENT INCLUSION MODEL 45
    Activity Three: Student Inclusion Gard Game 48
  THE FOUR QUADRANTS 56
    Discipline Orientation.. 57
    Activity Four: Discipline Orientation.......................... 59
    Learning Orientations 60
    Activity Five: Learning Orientations 63
    Personal Context 64
    Activity Six: Personal Context..................................... 67
    Social Context... 68
    Activity Seven: Social Context 70

WORKING WITH YOUR PERSONAS 71

  AN ILLUSTRATIVE EXAMPLE 71

EVALUATING STUDENT PROFILES 74

COURSE TEMPLATES AND ARTIFICIAL INTELLIGENCE 75

CONCLUSION 78

REFERENCES.. 79

List of Figures

Figure 1 - Frameworks in context   13
Figure 2 - ADDIE design approach   16
Figure 3 - Merrill's Principles of Instruction (MPI)   17
Figure 4 - Gagné, R. M., Briggs, L. J., & Wager, W. W. (1992). Principles of Instructional Design (redrawn)   19
Figure 5 - Atkinson's reinterpretation of Gagné's Steps into the 9S Model used at the Open Polytechnic of New Zealand.   20
Figure 6 - Bloom's Original 1956 Cognitive Domain Taxonomy   24
Figure 7 - Poster of Five Domains of Educational Objectives (A1 available at sijen.com)   24
Figure 8 - SOLE Model 'petals' aligned to the 8-SLDF   27
Figure 9 - An Excel Spreadsheet is used to plan and evaluate the design as it is created   28
Figure 10 - Structure of the DiAL-e (Burden and Atkinson 2009)   30
Figure 11 - Eight Stage Learning Design Framework: 8-SLDF (2016)   35
Figure 12 - Student Inclusion Model (after Thomas and May, 2010)   45
Figure 13 - The Four Quadrants   49
Figure 14 - Discipline Orientations   50
Figure 15 - Individual contexts   57
Figure 16 - Social Dimensions to Learning Cohorts   61

List of Tables

Table 1 - Student Characteristics based on Thomas and May (2010)   47
Table 2 - POISE Model   55

Author biography

Dr Simon Paul Atkinson is a social scientist, educational developer, and strategist with specialist interests in effective learning design and the application of educational technologies to teaching practice developed over 25 years' experience. He has been a Principal Fellow of the Higher Education Academy since 2015

His research interests focus on visualisations in support of academic practice. They also include tertiary education's strategic response to technology driven social change, the impact of technology-enabled communication on cultural interactions and the values of academe.

Formal roles have included Head of Learning and Development at Independent Schools of New Zealand, Manager of Learning Design at the Open Polytechnic of New Zealand, Associate Dean for Teaching and Learning (BPP University), Academic Developer (London School of Economics), Director of Teaching and Learning (Massey University - College of Education), Head of Centre for Learning Development (University of Hull), and Academic Developer (Open University UK).

Simon works as an Educational Strategic Consultant

His professional digital footprint starts at https://sijen.com

Preface

In 2022 I choose to start this series of eight short guides with stage four of my 8-Stage Learning Design Framework (8-SLDF), namely that stage dealing with writing effective learning outcomes. I had planned to produce the other seven stages in quick succession. However, life got in the way.

Circling back to the beginning with the first stage it becomes necessary to take up a little bit of the reader's time to outline the rationale for the framework. With apologies to those who have already read Writing Good Learning Outcomes and Objectives.

There is little training for new, or indeed existing, academics in our tertiary institutions on how to design effective courses and integrated programmes. This despite the growth in educational development units and the professionalisation of the tertiary teaching space. The emphasis is on teaching practice and assessment, rarely on course or programme design.

Academics with their knowledge expertise often teach retrospectively, trying to remember and mimic their own pathway through knowledge accumulation. I believe they need to take a holistic view of the learning design process to effectively design courses and programmes, or to work on their specific course within a defined structure.

This short volume introduces my eight-stage learning design framework (8-SLDF) and the first stage, the short-hand for which is 'Student Profiles'.

Dr Simon Paul Atkinson – 14 July 2024

Acknowledgements

I remain indebted to all the colleagues I have ever worked with for their insights, criticisms, and enthusiasm toward my approach to programme and course design. This includes colleagues at the Open University (UK), University of Hull, Massey University, London School of Economics and Political Sciences, BPP University and the Open Polytechnic of New Zealand.

Personal thanks go to Louise and Anna, both heartfelt friends who continue to share so much of their lives with me.

Last, and most definitely not least, to Dr Jeanette Atkinson, my wife, companion, best friend, and inspiration. Her love, support and patience sustain me through these passion projects, and through life.

Structure of this book

This work is intended as a guide to all those engaged in the process of constructing formal curricula. It is designed to be read through from beginning to end, although its subdivisions are designed to enable it to be used as both a handbook and as an instructional volume for those training academics.

It is subdivided into chapters which serve to build a persona or profile of the known, and unknown, student cohorts that will study your course or programme.

The book is divided into chapters, each of which is designed to be shared with your design team, or trainee teachers and designers, as the basis for discussion. Activities are suggested to facilitate some of that discussion.

My professional experience has been at tertiary level within formal educational provision, with polytechnics and universities in two English speaking countries, the United Kingdom, and New Zealand. The examples drawn upon inevitably reflect this socio-cultural context. However, the principles upon which the work rests are believed to be transferable to all formal learning contexts and to most non-formal provision, such as non-credit bearing adult learning programmes.

Given the desire for brevity, this short guide deals only with an overview of the 8-SLDF and stage one of the framework which relates to the creation of student profiles or personas.

British English spelling and grammar is used throughout.

We begin with an outline of the challenges faced by learning designers across all sectors, namely the rapidly evolving context in which design is occurring. Then we address the needs to orientate your design team, the need for everyone to be 'on the same page'.

We then explore the distinctions between frameworks, models and patterns of learning before outlining, briefly, some of the most popular approaches to learning design. These include ADDIE, Merrill's Principles of Instruction, Gagné's Nine Steps of Instruction (including my own reinterpretation), Universal Design for Learning (UDL), and Bloom's ever influential taxonomy. Also included are some more 'bespoke' and more recent approaches, my own SOLE Model and DiAL-e alongside the ABC, and 7c. All of these are not presented with critical commentary but rather serve to illustrate the fact that there are numerous different approaches.

The next section deals with the structure of the 8-SLDF, the Eight Stage Learning Design Framework. This necessitates a brief history and an outline of each of the eight stages to contextualise this, and future volumes.

Then we get to the meat of this stage, the creation of student personas or profiles. This explores three approaches, each arguably more penetrative and insightful than the last. Although, if you are just to adopt one, the Student Inclusion Model is a good place to start. The Four Quadrants Model provides further insight, and if you have design time, I think it makes sense to drill down using the POISE Model too.

The final two sections of the book explore how you work with your personas and evaluate them. I conclude with an observation about course templates and artificial intelligence, because at the time of writing this is pertinent, and I am frequently asked about it. I have no doubt that this section will age poorly. The rest of the book will stand the test of time though, I am sure.

The book is designed to serve as a guide or reader rather than as a workbook. However, there are activities which serve as prompts to reflection, and some questions to verify your understanding as you work through it.

There is a website that supports this work. This website can be accessed at:

https://sijen.com/

The Challenge of Course Design

All learning designers are essentially futurists.

This is because the student that embarks on your designed course will not develop the skills and attributes you have anticipated for them until a time when they have completed the course. If your course is part of a multi-year degree you can infer that you need to be thinking into a future that might be three or four years ahead.

This might seem like common sense, and to some extent it is, but we often do not start the design process with the kind of collective reflection that ensures we are the right people to design this course or programme. Whether we have the foresight and skills to anticipate what the future holds.

It is self-evident that if you have designed your course around practical activities using a piece of software, and you know that this version will inevitably be replaced several times in the next three years, you are likely to teach just the core and enduring functionalities of the software.

If you are teaching some aspect of urban planning, should you anticipate the impact of self-driving vehicles? When teaching a politics course on the Middle East, how well-grounded are your assumptions about the immoveable nature of borders.

Some of you might be saying, "But Simon, I teach history, or foundation level biology or mathematics.' You may have a point, but I stress 'may'. Perspectives on history change as new evidence is revealed, biology advances every day as technology provides new insights, and 'new' maths underpins much of the current Artificial Intelligence movement.

It is easier to teach about what is, rather than what might be. We owe it to our students to try. I ask only that you reflect on how much your discipline has changed in the last five or ten years.

Orientating your Design Team

It is important to establish the scope of this course or programme design. The canvas upon which it is being painted. The extent to which you must spend time doing this will depend on the experience of yourself and your design team members, and the consistency with which your institution plans and designs its courses. You may also benefit from an institution that has an experienced educational development unit that will assist you in your course designs.

In stages 2 and 3 of the 8-SLDF we will explore more broadly the context in which your course is being designed to ensure its optimal alignment to students' expectations and institutional capabilities. For now, we aim simply to ensure that we are setting off on the journey to design within our institutional limits.

There are several foundational questions that need to be answered by your team before you can begin. These include:

- What is the credit value of this course? (Most countries have nationally determined credit weightings for tertiary qualifications, in the form of 20 credits being equivalent to 200 hours of student learning, for example.
- Will your course fit into an existing programme that will otherwise be unchanged?
- If you are designing a new programme, what existing courses and pathways are anticipated?
- Will your offering be an option or a compulsory course?
- Will it have pre-requisites or post-requisites?

- What are the timetabling restraints – is there a formal pattern for learning delivery? It could be that the institutional expectation is for courses to be delivered through a 60-minute lecture and 120-minute seminar each week.
- Will it be available for out-of-programme enrolment? Some University courses are available for the public on a course-by-course basis.

Activity 1: Future Learning

Bring together a group of your colleagues who teach within the same discipline or programme as your course is being designed for.

This could be as few as two others and as many as you can fit into the room you are working in. Online there are no restrictions although for practical purposes I would suggest 15 as an upper limit.

Allow 30 minutes for this activity. You will need time later to reflect on what has been said. Doing this exercise online may be able to autogenerate a transcript which can be useful.

The deceptively simple question is:

What has changed in our discipline in the last five to ten years?

Asking the question as an historical one will inevitable turn to the present and future...trust me!

You may need to prompt colleagues by citing recent scholarly research, but it is more important to focus the conversation on societal changes because of recent developments in your discipline.

If you encounter any resistance you may want to ask a more pointed question, such as:

What impact do we think Artificial Intelligence will have on our discipline?

Design approaches: Frameworks, Patterns, Models and Philosophies

Experienced learning designers may already be aware of several other learning design approaches. Here we are going to explore some of the differences between them, without prejudice. You may already have a preferred design approach. You may still find value in incorporating aspects of the 8-SLDF into your practice. It is not an 'all-or-nothing' framework.

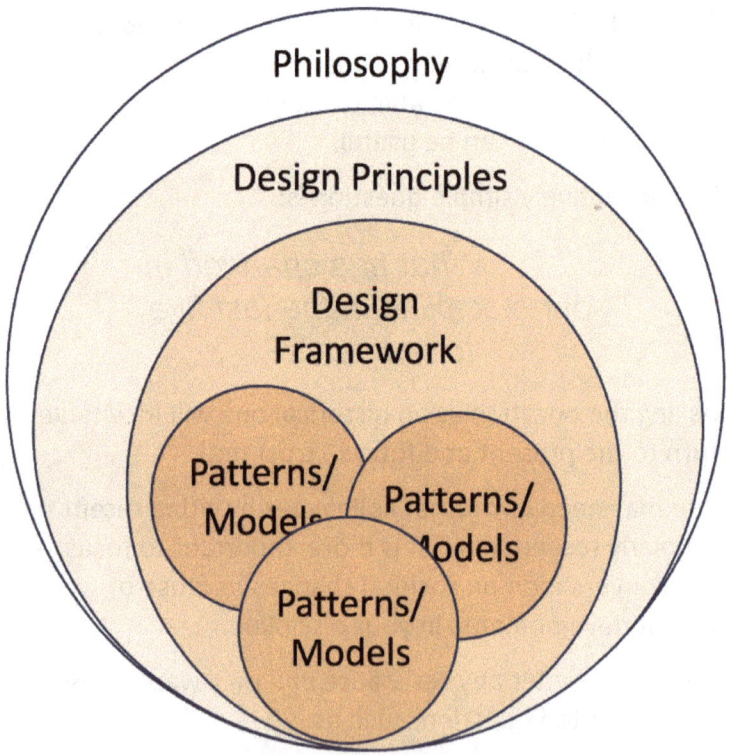

Figure 1 - Frameworks in context

It is important to differentiate between programme and course design frameworks and learning activity pattern designs. The web is awash with sites, often from learning development units in universities that merge both approaches under the banner of instructional design models. For instructional you may substitute the words learning or educational. I am going to identify a few of each category, frameworks and patterns, and I trust next time you encounter any purported 'model' you will be able to identify which form it takes.

Frameworks are holistic, they take a bird's eye view of the entire learning journey and ensure the course, and the programme that fits within it, is coherent and as effective to teach and learn as possible.

Patterns are designed at the level of a specific learning activity, or a series of activities. This could be a pattern for the learning delivery of an entire course or part of an individual session.

Frameworks are therefore best seen as defining the course or programme design, whereas a pattern is concerned with learning delivery.

Let us take a few of the most often cited 'models', ADDIE (Analysis, Design, Development, Implementation, and Evaluation), Gagné's Nine Steps for Instruction, Merrill's Principles of Instruction (MPI), Universal Design for Learning (UDL), and Bloom's (Cognitive) Taxonomy.

ADDIE

ADDIE is one of the more ubiquitous models, heavily used by professional development and e-learning professionals (Branch, 2009). At its simplest it is simply a five stage of course design approach, to be followed in sequence A-D-D-I-E, (with some iterative loops allowed) of analysis, design, development, implementation, and evaluation.

Even a cursory glance makes clear this framework (See Figure 1) does not fully articulate what is to happen within each of these five stages. Indeed, it is presented as a design model by many even though its second step is the ill-defined 'design'.

As we will explore later, the 8-SLDF unpicks the design stage within ADDIE into a four stage 'loop'. Where ADDIE does have strength in suggesting that course designers need to give thought to the live implementation of designs, their impact on staff and students

At best ADDIE could be described as a design framework, although I tend to put it in the same list as other project management approaches.

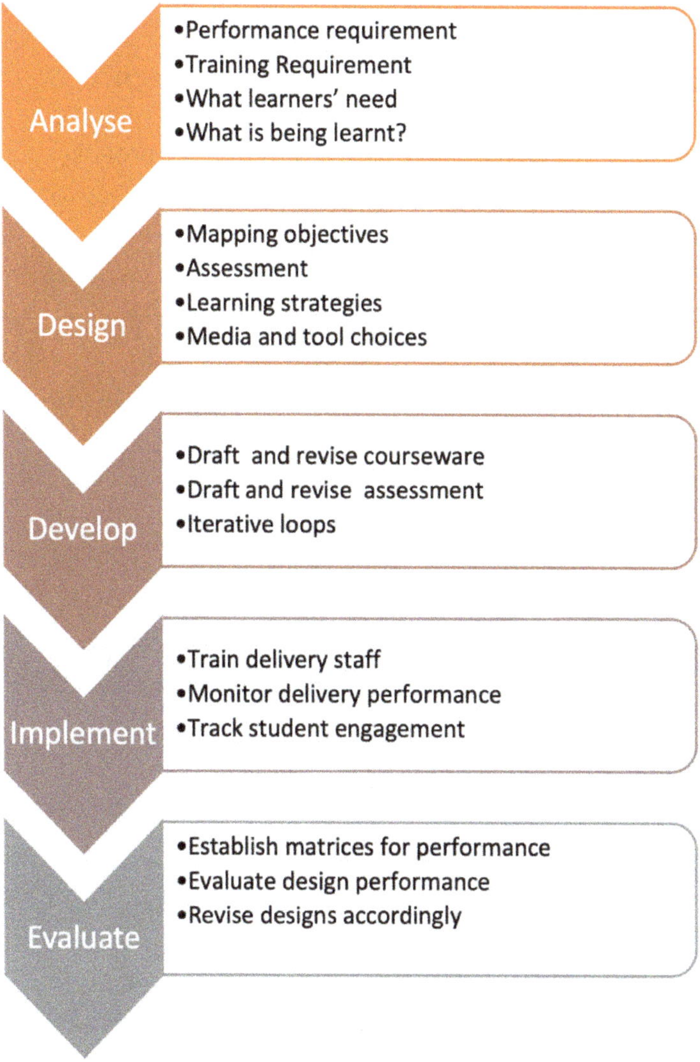

Analyse
- Performance requirement
- Training Requirement
- What learners' need
- What is being learnt?

Design
- Mapping objectives
- Assessment
- Learning strategies
- Media and tool choices

Develop
- Draft and revise courseware
- Draft and revise assessment
- Iterative loops

Implement
- Train delivery staff
- Monitor delivery performance
- Track student engagement

Evaluate
- Establish matrices for performance
- Evaluate design performance
- Revise designs accordingly

Figure 2 - ADDIE design approach

Merrill's Principles of Instruction (MPI)

Merrill's Principles of Instruction (MPI) is a set of design principles, not a framework (Merrill, 2013). It aims to support appropriate task-centred pattern approaches.

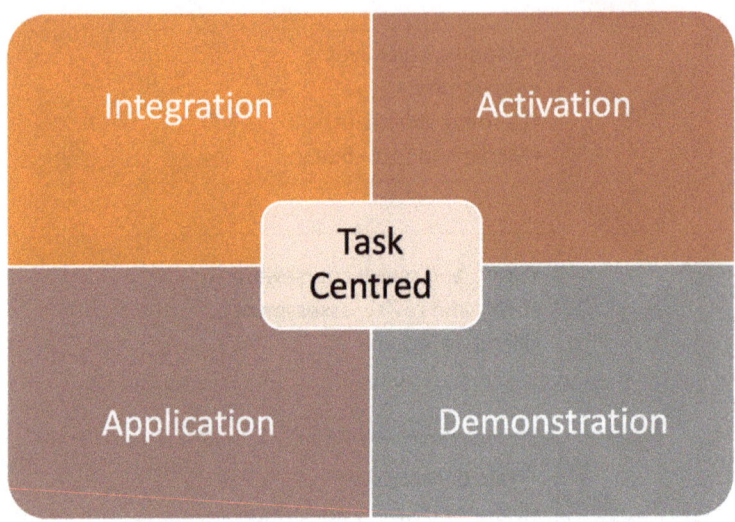

Figure 3 - Merrill's Principles of Instruction (MPI)

MPI has five principles:
- Task-centred: Learning requires the development of problem solving and critical thinking skills applied to authentic real-world experiences
- Activation: Learning occurs when learners activate relevant cognitive structures, stimulating recall.
- Demonstration: Learning occurs when learners observe demonstrations of the skills to be learnt.
- Application: Learning occurs when learners apply newly acquired knowledge and skills and receive feedback on their performance.

- Integration: Learning occurs when learning is integrated into daily practice.

For faculty and learning activity designers, Merrill's Principles serves to enable the design of engaging, relevant, and practical instructional activities. It simply articulates the cognitive process through which most learning is acquired.

It is an interactive set of principles and useful as an internal evaluative approach in designing any learning activity. It helps to answer the often-unspoken question in a student's mind, 'why am I being asked to do this?" Being able to work through the five principles at a task level, or perhaps at an individual learning session level (lecture, seminar, or webinar) helps ensure the learning is serving its intended purpose.

Merrill's Principles are not a course or programme design framework. It could be adopted across an entire course to articulate the nature of the learning delivery, but it is not a framework in and of itself.

Gagné's Nine Steps for Instruction

Robert Gagné's Nine Steps for Instruction does apply to individual activity design and can be abstracted to reflect the entire course design structure, but it is still not a design framework (Gagné et al., 1992; Gagné & Driscoll, 1988). I see it as a design pattern. It is focussed on what happens when a student is directly engaged in the learning experience rather than in the broader context of the course or programme design.

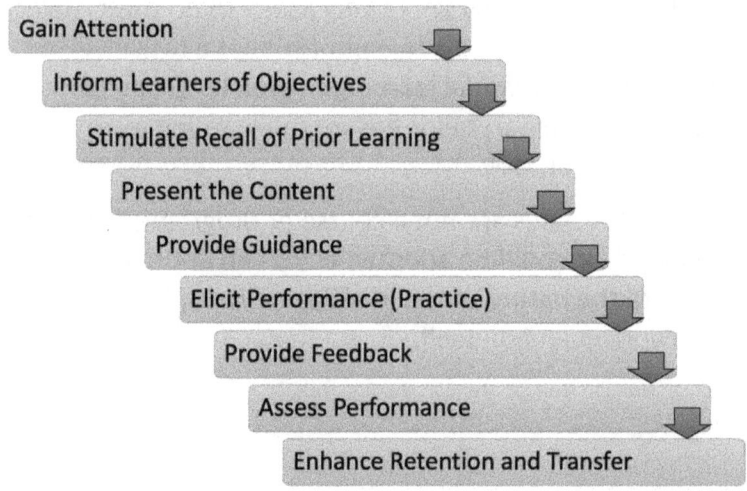

Figure 4 - Gagné, R. M., Briggs, L. J., & Wager, W. W. (1992). Principles of Instructional Design (redrawn)

It is a useful pattern of learning design that I used at the Open Polytechnic NZ as Manager of Learning Design to support the design of learning activities within a course, and to influence the structure of the course, formalising the learning stages at the point of delivery.

To make it more accessible and memorable, I renamed each stage. With an S word, creating the '9S model', and this was aligned to an indigenous approach to learning articulated in 10 (later 12) Learning Design Principles.

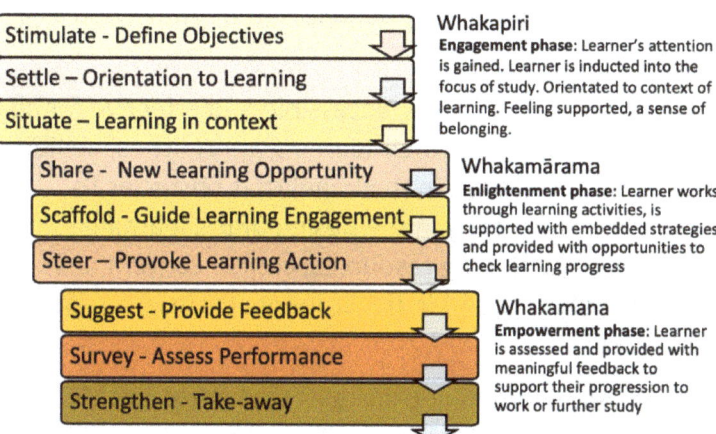

Figure 5 - Atkinson's reinterpretation of Gagné's Steps into the 9S Model used at the Open Polytechnic of New Zealand.

The 9S was used to design weekly patterns of learning activity, although the wider course design process was dictated by project management approaches, using a form of 'agile' development. This was somewhat frustrating on a personal level as I believed this created disconnected learning, quite the opposite of its intention. The reason I believe this happened was that an 'agile' project methodology, without referencing a design framework, made it too easy to lose sight of the fundamental nature of the learners for whom the courses were intended.

It is a reminder that there are always going to be institutional processes that can get in the way of your good design intentions.

Universal Design for Learning - UDL

One of the most attractive, and aspirational, design concepts in education has been that of Universal Design for Learning or UDL. It is less a pattern or a framework, rather it is a philosophy, though it is frequently cited as a framework.

UDL aims to make learning accessible and effective for all students, regardless of their learning approaches, abilities or backgrounds. Based in the belief that obstacles to learning are frequently in the design of the learning environment (including resources, course content and modes of delivery), not in the students themselves (Sewell et al., 2022).

UDL has three dominant principles that designers should facilitate in their designs: multiple means of engagement, multiple means of representation, and multiple means of action and expression.

This has a positive effect of promoting inclusive learning environments by accommodating diverse learning styles and needs. This is particularly beneficial to learning difficulties. It is also arguably a form of flexible learning, allowing students to gravitate to a particular pattern of engagement that serves their personal learning approach. Where UDL extends the choice of learning pathways there is also evidence that students' levels of engagement are enhanced, and academic performance is also improved.

One of the most powerful effects of merely considering the principles of UDL in any design team is it facilitates teachers' acknowledgement of their students' unique learning preferences and needs.

There are some downsides to UDL too. Done properly it is both time consuming and resource intensive. Certainly, those who are unfamiliar with the approach or using it in a new institutional context will find it just how many invisible roadblocks they will encounter within existing processes.

Implemented at scale, UDL requires significant institutional commitment, not least in training and professional development. This is true not only of the learning designers and teaching staff, but also to those engaged in marking and assessment, as well as student support.

UDL presents some challenges for its effective deployment, but its aspirations are worth taking account of.

Bloom's (Cognitive) Taxonomy

Bloom's (Cognitive) Taxonomy has been the enduring contribution of Bloom and his colleagues from the 1950s (Bloom, 1956). I added the 'cognitive' above to specify that Bloom's Taxonomy usually refers to just this single domain, although Bloom's team also developed taxonomies for affective (emotional/values) (Krathwohl et al., 1956) and psychomotor (practical/manual) learning (Dave, 1967).

These taxonomies are neither design frameworks nor patterns. Nor do they represent an underlying philosophy. Bloom's teams developed categorisations of identified behaviours, assembled them into a hierarchy which have ever since been used to develop 'copies' of these stages of development.

They are a tool designed, informed by sound educational psychological observations, that support the reflective processes of teachers and designers. Such taxonomies ensure learning activities are pitched at the right level and can, by use of further instrumentation, support the use of any pattern design approach.

'Bloom's Taxonomy' has been widely adopted (without reference to the broader scope of the original work) as a means of categorising and ordering thinking skills. It serves as a categorisation from lower (bottom) to higher (top) learning skills.

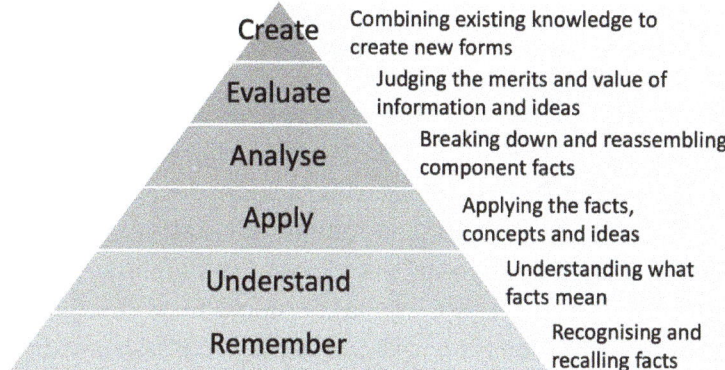

Figure 6 - Bloom's Original 1956 Cognitive Domain Taxonomy

Very often represented as a pyramid, more recent representations, including my own, favour a circle, allowing additional outer rings to be added for assessment and task ideas.

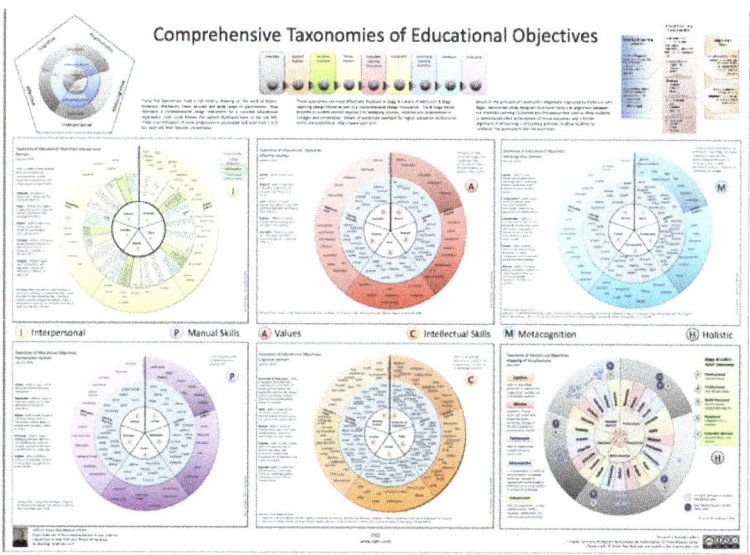

Figure 7 - Poster of Five Domains of Educational Objectives (A1 available at sijen.com)

There is a section on Educational Taxonomies at stage four of the 8-SLDF (Atkinson, 2022) so I will not go into detail here as to how they inform my, or my design teams, approaches. Suffice it to say that I have made significant use of these educational taxonomies, adaptations of the three original Bloom Team's work and my own metacognitive and interpersonal domains. I use these to ensure intended learning outcomes are progressive within a course or programme, and that they are assessable.

Other Approaches

There are any number of other approaches, all of which I believe fall into the category of learning design patterns, rather than as course design frameworks. Some of these we will revisit in more detail in stage 6 of the framework 'Learning and Teaching Activities', so they are only outlined briefly in the pages that follow.

These include my own SOLE model (Atkinson, 2011b), and the DIAL-e Framework developed with Kevin Burden (Burden & Atkinson, 2009), both named before I chose to articulate the differences between frameworks and patterns!

You may find that your institution, regional or national authority, or other determining institution, has a preferred model of learning activity design.

The beauty of the 8-SLDF is it is relatively neutral as to the learning and teaching activity approach you take. In postgraduate education I have favoured the SOLE model, in vocational undergraduate design I have used the 9S model. I do not believe in a rigid 'one size fits all approach'.

SOLE (Student Owned Learning Engagement) model

The SOLE (Student Owned Learning Engagement) model was designed to ensure students were exposed to a broad range of learning activities, in the spirit of Universal Design for Learning (see below). These were not alternative modes of the same learning, rather they were intended to ensure balance in the kinds of learning that students were exposed to.

The SOLE models aim is to give autonomy to the learner, calibrating their efforts around notional student hours. It is fair to say that the prime motivation for developing the model was student, and staff, workload concerns.

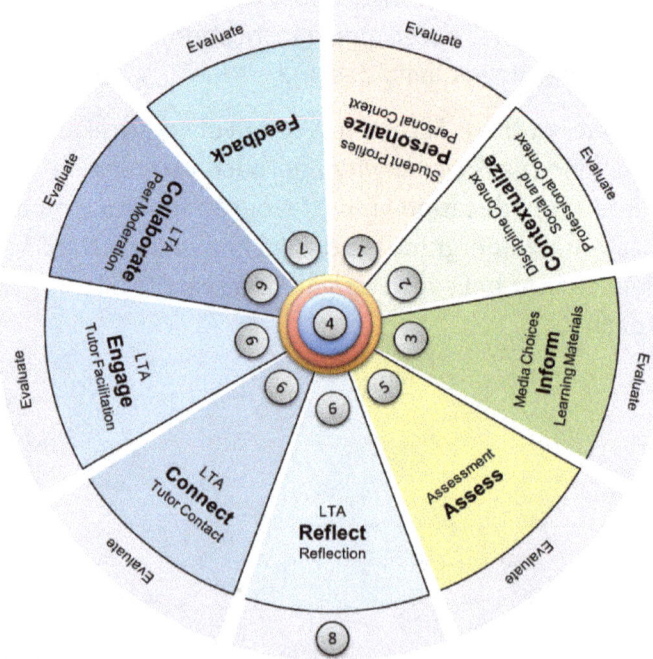

Figure 8 - SOLE Model 'petals' aligned to the 8-SLDF

The model has nine dimensions (or petals) in the model, each aligned to a range of educational theory and practice. In this illustration each petal also references the wider 8-SLDF. This will be revisited when we explore stage 6 'Learning and Teaching Activity Design'.

The model is intended to ensure coverage of learning content and to ensure that students are being given an appropriate workload. It is a practical model that has an associated toolkit, an open Excel spreadsheet (available at sijen.com), that allows design teams to track student effort, balance of activity type and potentially the cost of development.

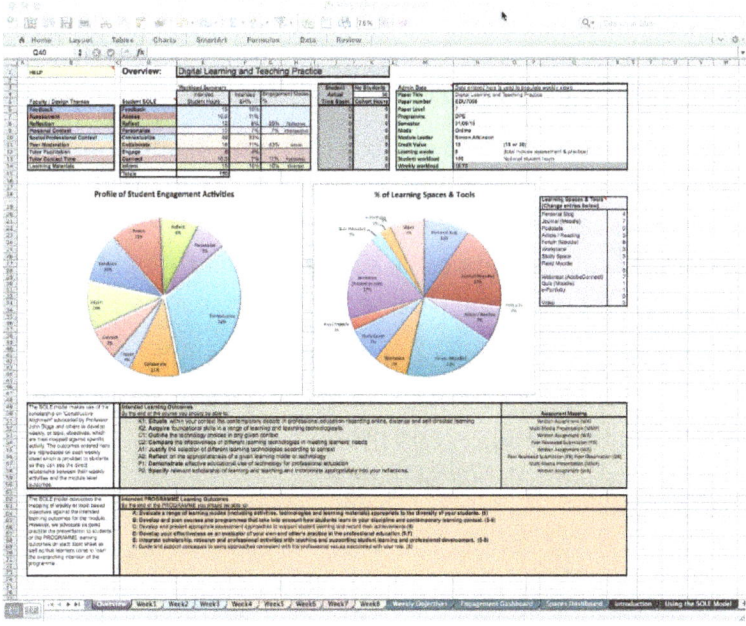

Figure 9 - An Excel Spreadsheet is used to plan and evaluate the design as it is created

DIAL-e (Digital Artifacts for Learner Engagement) Framework

The Dial-e 'framework' is a series of lesson patterns developed as part of a JISC funded project in the UK between 2006-2008. It was conceived of as a "proof of concept" project, leveraging the growing number of digital repositories. These included newsreel and video archives, cartoon and newspaper collections and maps.

Professor Kevin Burden and I developed a series of learning patterns based on existing classroom and online teaching practices. We provided illustrations and exemplars using an archive of newsreels, later with examples using cartons and maps. There was an interactive resource on a JISC service, now discontinued, but there remain examples on YouTube.

Some of the patterns have more than one example and we tried to illustrate them with a diverse range of media. Its power was serving to shift the mindset of academics from thinking about content to be served, to the thought process students were expected to exercise.

The DiAL-e was not radical, but it did beautifully respond to the academics' inclination to teach content range rather than learning strategies and presented an alternative way of engaging with all digital media.

Pattern	Mode	Spaces				
Stimulation	Engagement	Independent	Active / Mobile	Small Groups / Seminars	Large Groups / Lectures	Online – Distance Learning
Narrative	Engagement					
Authoring	Engagement					
Empathising	Engagement					
Collaboration	Knowledge Construction					
Conceptualisation	Knowledge Construction					
Enquiry	Knowledge Construction					
Research	Reflection					
Representation	Reflection					
Figurative	Reflection					

Figure 10 - Structure of the DiAL-e (Burden and Atkinson 2009)

ABC Learning Design

The ABC Learning Design approach, developed at University College London (UCL) (Young & Perović, 2016), is designed as a rapid, collaborative method for designing learning activities and curricula. Deploying storyboards as a way of constructing the learner's journey, mapping out the sequence of learning activities aiming to achieve constructive alignment.

The ABC model describes six learning types, more accurately to be defined as types of activity, that are broadly aligned to Professor Diana Laurillard's conversational framework (Laurillard, 2002). These six activity types are: acquisition, collaboration, discussion, investigation, practice, and production.

One of the attractions of the ABC approach is that it reports successful faculty engagement through 'high-energy' workshops lasting just 90 minutes in which teaching teams design and redesign their courseware. This collaborative approach works particularly well where team-teaching is a feature. Once faculty and designers go through the process a few times they become very adept at maximising the flexibility inherent in the approach. It certainly has the attractiveness, as does the SOLE model and DIAL-e Framework of encouraging a diverse range of learning activities.

As with any thoughtful design approach it can be resource intensive, although the short duration of each design workshop can be attractive to management. The onus is on the coordinator to prepare materials and resources in advance.

The project team's website is: https://blogs.ucl.ac.uk/abc-ld/

7C's

The **7C's approach to learning design** is intended to guide educational designers in creating effective and engaging learning experiences (Conole, 2014). The 7c's consists of seven key elements: Conceptualize, Capture, Create, Communicate, Collaborate, Consider, and Consolidate.

1. **Conceptualize**: This initial stage involves defining the learning objectives, understanding the learners' needs, and outlining the overall structure of the learning experience.//
2. **Capture**: In this phase, educators gather and organise resources, including content, tools, and materials that will be used in the learning process.
3. **Create**: This step focuses on designing and developing the actual learning activities and materials, ensuring they align with the learning objectives.
4. **Communicate**: Effective communication strategies are established to facilitate interaction between learners and instructors, as well as among learners themselves.
5. **Collaborate**: This component emphasises the importance of collaborative learning, encouraging group work and peer-to-peer interactions.
6. **Consider**: Reflection and assessment are key in this stage, where educators evaluate the effectiveness of the learning activities and make necessary adjustments.
7. **Consolidate**: Finally, the learning design is implemented and evaluated in a real learning context and refined based on feedback and evaluation.

The 7c's aims to provide a reflective structure that operates at a programme and course level, much as the 8-SLDF does. Although I believe step 3 is too loosely defined to ensure constructive alignment is ensured.

Nonetheless it does provide a systematic approach to designing learning experiences. Having learner engagement at its heart, well used effectively it produces well-structured learning. Developed in the UK university sector it also risks making some resource assumptions. As always access to resources and the need for training of design teams need to be accounted for.

The 7C's approach to learning design offers a robust and flexible framework that can enhance the quality of education, though it does come with some challenges related to time and resource requirements.

Activity 2: Design Approaches

Gather your design team together or find a handful of willing colleagues or senior students in the absence of an established team.

Consider what existing delivery patterns exist within your institution and ask whether you are restricted by them. Will an alternative approach risk encountering challenges at validation? How much 'wriggle room' do you have?

Consider whether you are designing from the beginning, or whether there is already a template for courses and programmes within which you are compelled to design.

Remember that many of the patterns outlined above are the focus on stage 6 of the 8-SLDF, that deals with learning and teaching activities and can be contained within the 8-SLDF framework.

The chances are your design journey can be independent (and very worthwhile) even if the final output needs to conform to a bureaucratic form.

At this point you are simply exploring design options.

8-Stage Learning Design Framework

The 8-Stage Learning Design Framework, or 8-SLDF for short, is designed to be a supportive guide, step by step, enabling faculty and course designers, and their teams, to develop high quality, enduring yet flexible, well-aligned programmes or courses.

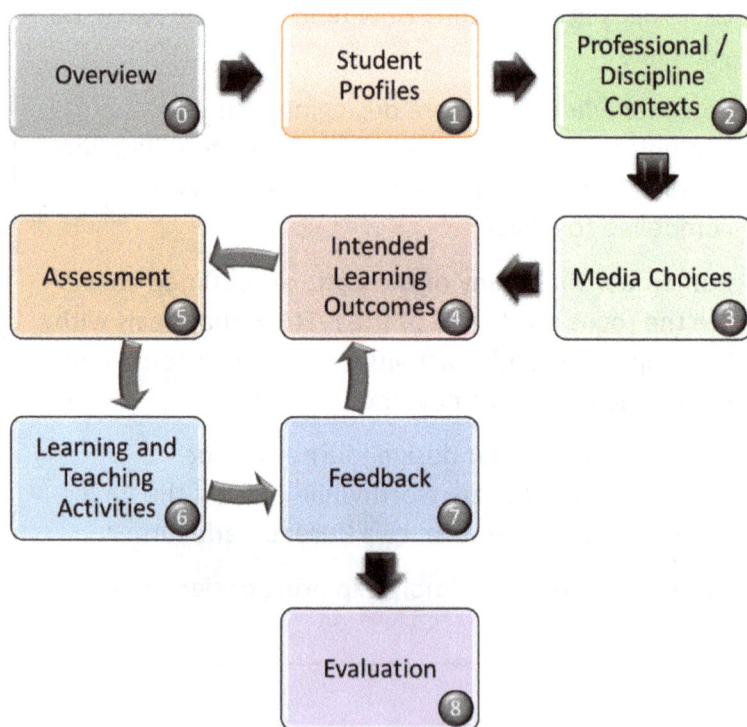

Figure 11 - Eight Stage Learning Design Framework: 8-SLDF (2016)

Very Brief History

The 8-Stage Learning Design Framework has had a long gestation beginning with my work at the Open University (UK) in the early 2000s.

I was impressed by the earlier work done by Derek Rowntree (1994) and Fred Lockwood (1994) in outlining the design principles of distance learning materials in a predominately paper-based environment. I later encountered the progressive insights of Tony Bates, originally published in 1984 (2016), that explored the role of technology in distance education.

The foundation of the 8-SLDF lies in my educational development practice, sharing the insights and approaches of work done by John Biggs on constructive alignment (Biggs & Tang, 2007) and the SOLO taxonomy (Biggs & Collis, 1982). Later as I got frustrated with the narrow obsession of tertiary educators around Bloom's cognitive domain, I incorporated the work of Anderson and Krathwohl's reworking of Bloom's cognitive domain taxonomy (2001) alongside others domain development, notably the original Bloom project's articulation of the Affective domain (1956), Dave's psychomotor domain (1967), and my own interpretations of Metacognitive and Interpersonal domains. These taxonomies served to underpin the writing of effective intended learning outcomes.

By 2006 the issue of effective learning material design, inspired by the pre-digital distance learning world, influenced my collaborations with Kevin Burden around the DiAL-e Framework (Burden & Atkinson, 2009) and my own scholarship around the SOLE Model (Atkinson, 2011a).

Later I drew inspiration from the work of James Dalziel (2016), and Diana Laurillard (Laurillard, 2012) in their learning design conceptualisations, specifically as these related to the design of learning activities.

The result, the 8-SLDF, is a comprehensive, flexible and adaptable learning design framework. It is suitable for entire courses, modules and programmes. It is a framework that applies to any discipline, level, context or mode of learning. It is a framework for any adult, formal, learning context.

Summary of the Eight Stages

Understanding the broader context in which designing student profiles and personas is important, so it is appropriate to spend a little time reviewing all eight stages within the 8-SLDF.

Overview – Learning Philosophy

Well-designed courses are the only way of ensuring that students and faculty can both engage in learning collaboration that is meaningful, positive and fruitful.

A well-designed course is one that is constructively aligned, relevant to the current and future real-world experiences of students, and is stimulating, engaging and transparent.

Constructively aligned simply means there are clearly defined intended learning outcomes, that these are what is assessed, and that the learning and teaching activities are guided by these.

Transparent means that any student choosing to take this course or programme is provided with a clear map of the learning journey they are embarking upon. Written in a language that is suitable for someone before they embark on the course or programme, the student should be able to anticipate the intellectual and personal challenges that awaits them.

Any course and programme must also be cultural and socially aware. Too often educators neglect to state what to them is obvious, this course on x is being taught from y perspective. Unless all your students are exactly like you, from identical backgrounds, socio-economic status, religious conviction, linguistic ability, you should never assume that the individual's orientation to the subject or discipline is a shared one.

Part of transparency is ensuring that students know why they are being asked to perform specific learning tasks. We as faculty and designers should always have an answer to the question of 'why' an activity matters. Sharing with the student the reasoning behind including any learning activity, is the first step towards an individual's self-reflective process, their metacognition, and the development of their personal epistemologies (Atkinson, 2014).

Students also deserve to know 'why' because doing anything for the sake of it is clearly wasteful of their time.

The final reason for wanting to create well-designed courses is to reflect the fact that we, as faculty, are crucial players in the relationship between our students, the discipline, our institution and the wider world. Being good at designing courses makes us and our colleagues' better teachers. Designing courses that enable us all to better at what we do simply makes sense.

Stage 1: Designing for Students: Personas and Profiles

This obviously is the focus of this volume so will be outlined just briefly here.

Courses, entire programmes or individual modules, are designed to reflect our institutional specialisms and priorities but we sometimes risk forgetting that they will be taken by flesh-and-blood students! Profiling students' learning orientations is challenging. In this volume we will explore students' educational, circumstantial, dispositional and cultural orientations for learning. We will discuss practical interpretations of the scholarship about personal epistemologies to design courses that are best suited to the intended students (Atkinson, 2014).

Stage 2: Designing for Professional or Discipline Contexts

Tertiary providers are increasingly expected to deliver 'work-ready' graduates. This is a challenge when we must acknowledge that many graduates will begin a career in a few years' time that does not exist today. Identifying the competency frameworks within our disciplines and those of our professional colleagues is a good place to start (Atkinson, 2015). We can then identify a range of graduate attributes that will underpin our programme outcomes and inform the development of real-world assessment.

We may not know exactly what the future of our discipline might look like. We can look backwards and draw conclusions about its most probable path going into the future.

Stage 3: Media Choices Informing Design

Students' expectations with respect to the digital formats, accessibility and flexibility of learning materials and communication channels have put enormous pressure on institutions. Many have relied on a single centralised digital ecosystem, often a Virtual Learning Environment (VLE) by some name or other and continue to wrestle with the ubiquitous nature of Wifi and handheld devices.

In this 8-SLDF stage designers identify the media needs of their students, both in terms of what is currently provided and what graduates might expect to meet in their future practice. Media refers to the tools as much as to the content. Designing courses in a flexible manner using appropriate media, and justifying those decisions to students, secures greater engagement.

Stage 4: Writing Good Learning Outcomes and Objectives

After designers have orientated themselves to the notion of constructive alignment and level differentiation, an exploration of the use of educational taxonomies across five domains of learning serve to draft well-structured intended learning outcomes (ILOs).

These will be appropriate to the aims of the module and programme and take account of their need to be assessable. They will also be drafted to reflect the needs of the disciplines or professions your graduates are intending to pursue.

Stage 5: Developing a Meaningful Assessment Strategy

Knowing what the ILOs are, enables designers to craft meaningful assessments that provide opportunities to students to evidence their learning against those ILOs.

At this stage of the 8-SLDF designers identify which outcomes can be combined across different domains of learning to manage the assessment load, for both faculty and student, whilst ensuring all ILOs are assessed.

Drafting marking rubrics for the appropriate level that represent all the guidance that individual assessors and students need to guide their practice completes this stage.

Stage 6: Designing Engaging Learning Opportunities

The third element in a constructively aligned course design are the learning activities that allow students to prepare for the assessment of their learning outcomes.

This stage is not about the content that we share with our students, it is about how students are engaged with that content. Some modules or courses will require a good deal of knowledge to be acquired by novice learners and a set-text and lectures may be the appropriate strategy. Is knowledge accumulation important at this level?

Alternatively, we might be designing a more advanced module in which a discovery learning approach is more appropriate. We may choose to develop an inquiry-based learning models here instead, asking our students to prepare to take a debate position, run a Moot or team-based discussion? The important thing at this stage is that designers are developing a strategy and practical approaches that build on their design, not seeking innovation for innovation's sake.

Stage 7: Creating Opportunities for Feedback Throughout

The fourth element in a constructively aligned course design approach is feedback throughout.

Reflective of both our assessment practice and our learning activities, feedback is best fully integrated into the learning rather than seen as a separate administrative response to submitted work.

Designing feedback throughout opportunities in our courses will lead us to adopt variations in our learning activities and potentially to modify our assessment strategies too. There is no point in assessing students in a form that has not allowed them to rehearse for such assessment.

Identifying how to give feedback on preparatory activities acts as a litmus test for sound assessment. It also allows us to identify fresh approaches to learning activities.

Stage 8: In-course and Post Course Evaluation Strategies

It may seem strange to design evaluation structures before you have even recruited students onto your courses or programmes.

We need first to understand the importance of both the evaluation for-learning and the evaluation of-learning. It is important to ensure that we have efficient and effective in-course evaluation techniques already in mind to make sure there is an opportunity to enhance the course as it is underway. We need to avoid making knee-jerk adjustments to a module that appears not to be working.

Most institutions' end-of-module evaluation processes do not generate actionable data. We can design-in some of our own.

In-course evaluation needs to be appropriately positioned within a course, with the correct amount of time and preparation allowed. We also need to decide in advance where we anticipate the enhancement opportunities are for our course and design post-course evaluation instruments to capture them.

If you want to follow this framework online, bookmark: https://sijen.com/research-interests/8-stage-learning-design-framework.

Stage 1: Student Profiles or Personas

Courses, whether entire programmes or individual courses, reflect our institutional specialisms and priorities, social and economic priorities. and often our own interests. We sometimes risk forgetting that they will be taken by future cohorts of flesh-and-blood students. The fact that they are individuals within a future cohort is significant.

Being able to anticipate the range of learning orientations and dispositions, approaches to learning, and relationship with the discipline among your future students is challenging. Developing meaningful student personas or profiles, I am going to use the term persona from now on, takes a little time but is foundational. It ensures you and your team are designing for students, not for the content knowledge itself.

The intention is not to create a single archetype or to stereotype your students. Each individual student brings with them a personal history, a personal story. There is nonetheless value in identifying trends in who is likely to form the student cohort of your future course or programme.

This enables us to ensure modules and programmes are designed to meet students' expectations, capabilities and learning intentions. Well-designed courses save a lot of supplemental support and future adjustments along the way.

There are two overlapping approaches to generate a meaningful set of student personas. You may choose to do any of them, a part of them, or a variation on all of them, the important thing is that you reach beyond simply describing your existing student cohort.

1. Student Inclusion Model
2. Learning Orientations

Student Inclusion Model

This approach makes use of a range of student characteristics drawn from Thomas and May's work on inclusion (Thomas & May, 2010). It serves to explore a wide range of pre-conditions that may be part of any cohort. Unless you are teaching clones, there will always be variation within your cohort.

You do not need to create unique learning experiences for each individual student, while recognising that that is precisely what happens. Every student will have a unique personal experience of your course or programme.

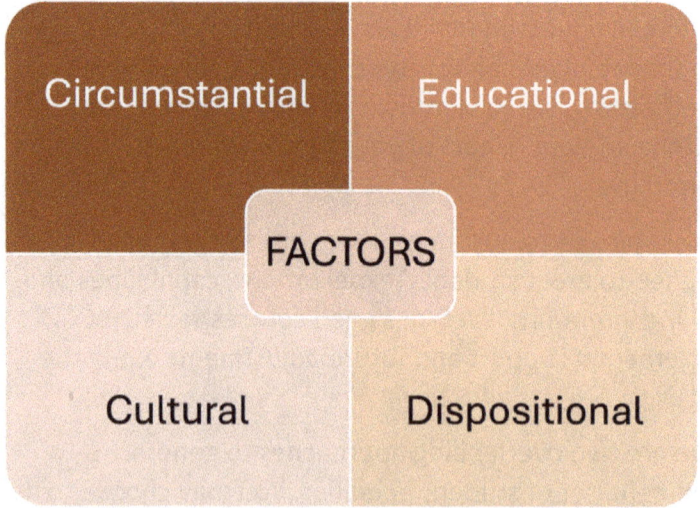

Figure 12 - Student Inclusion Model (after Thomas and May, 2010)

Exploring students' educational, circumstantial, dispositional and cultural orientations for learning, will help you broaden your concept of who your students are. Later we will explore a deeper model to examine the potential personal epistemologies of our students, how they believe knowledge happens. For now, we are going to sketch out a huge range of variables that might illustrate the potential diversity we might face as teachers and as learning designers.

Circumstantial	Age; disability; paid/voluntary employment; caring responsibilities; geographical location; access to IT; access to transport services; time availability; financial background and means; marital status.
Educational	Level/type of entry qualifications; unique skills; evident abilities; breadth of knowledge; educational experience; life and work experience; learning approaches (preferences); educational history; international experiences; identifiable learning needs.

Cultural	Written language abilities; spoken language abilities; personal values; cultural capital; religion and belief; country of origin/residence; ethnicity/race; social background; individualism vs collectivism; extracurricular activities.
Dispositional	Confidence; motivation; aspirations; expectations; attitudes; epistemological beliefs; emotional intelligence; maturity; self-awareness; gender and sexuality.

Table 1 - Student Characteristics modified from Thomas and May (2010)

Activity Three: Student Inclusion Gard Game

This can be a challenging but enjoyable 'game'.

The intention is to create between four and eight personas based on a range of factors.

The convenor will already have prepared several cards. The next few pages have my versions. You can photocopy these (maybe expand them to A4).

Each has just one or two words based around Thomas and May's characteristics. Each card is colour coded to identify it as a facet of educational, circumstantial, dispositional or cultural disposition.

You may choose to debate the meaning or scope of each characteristic so that everyone eon the team is speaking the same language

Shuffle these cards and then deal each person as many each as it takes to use them all up.

Each person must then use just one, two or three words to identify that characteristic in its personified form. For example, I am dealt the card that reads "Access to IT" so I write "Superfast Broadband User". Someone eels receiving the same card might have written "Uses Library PCs".

The point is that when every card is annotated, they are gathered in again and redealt with a similar number from each disposition.

The result is an often amusing but, importantly, diverse range of personas.

Write these up on the board and remember to take a photograph at the end of the workshop

AGE	DISABILITY
Circumstantial	Circumstantial
PAID/VOLUNTARY EMPLOYMENT	CARING RESPONSABILITIES
Circumstantial	Circumstantial
GEOGRAPHICAL LOCATION	ACCESS TO IT
Circumstantial	Circumstantial

ACCESS TO TRANSPORT SERVICES	TIME AVAILABILITY
Circumstantial	Circumstantial
FINANCIAL BACKGROUND	**MARITAL STATUS**
Circumstantial	Circumstantial
ENTRY QUALIFICATIONS	**UNIQUE SKILLS**
Educational	Educational

EVIDENT ABILITIES	BREADTH OF KNOWLEDGE
Educational	Educational

EDUCATIONAL EXPERIENCE	LIFE AND WORK EXPERIENCE
Educational	Educational

LEARNING APPROACHES	EDUCATIONAL HISTORY
Educational	Educational

INTERNATIONAL EXPERIENCES	IDENTIFIABLE LEARNING NEEDS
Educational	Educational
CONFIDENCE	MOTIVATION
Dispositional	Dispositional
ASPIRATIONS	EXPECTATIONS
Dispositional	Dispositional

ATTITUDES	EPISTEMOLOGICAL BELIEFS
Dispositional	Dispositional
EMOTIONAL INTELLIGENCE	MATURITY
Dispositional	Dispositional
SELF-AWARENESS	GENDER AND SEXUALITY
Dispositional	Dispositional

WRITTEN LANGUAGE ABILITIES	SPOKEN LANGUAGE ABILITIES
Cultural	Cultural
PERSONAL VALUES	CULTURAL CAPITAL
Cultural	Cultural
RELIGION AND BELIEFS	COUNTRY OF ORIGIN / RESIDENCE
Cultural	Cultural

ETHNICITY / RACE	SOCIAL BACKGROUND
Cultural	Cultural
INDIVIDUALISM vs COLLECTIVISM	EXTRACURRICULAR ACTIVITIES
Cultural	Cultural

You can choose to create your own versions of these cards to reflect your terminological context, but my advice is to be as broad as possible and not to get too hung up on specific definitions.

The Four Quadrants

Another approach is to embark on a collegial conversation around four different quadrants that impact on the student experience, two might be termed orientations and two contexts.

You can choose to discuss any one of these full first. There is certainly an argument to say that you can start at any point in the quadrant and arrive at a significant conclusion. It is important that all four orientations are discussed.

This is not a mechanical process, you cannot feed data in, and an ideal student profile pops out the other end, but it is highly effective in orientating your course or programme design towards meeting you future students' needs.

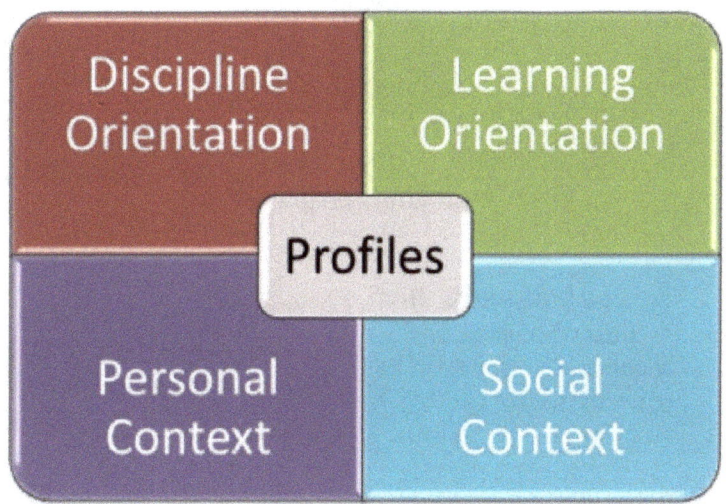

Figure 13 - The Four Quadrants

Discipline Orientation

Why start with a profile of your discipline? It must be obvious, surely? You are educating the future thinkers and contributors to your discipline, and you would want them to see its value the way you do.

That might be a little self-indulgent, but we know from experience that students very often start their programme with fundamental misconceptions about the discipline. We should never take for granted that how we understand our discipline is shared by our students.

Asking ourselves four deceptively simple questions as a design team is a good place to start.

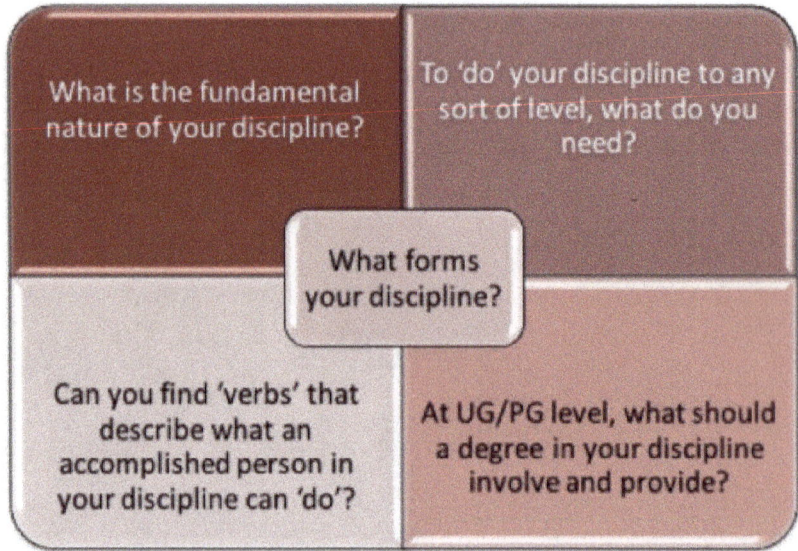

Figure 14 - Discipline Orientations

1) What is the fundamental nature of your discipline?
    a) What do students think this discipline is all about?
    b) Is it essentially a reflective or analytical discipline?

c) Principally qualitative or quantitative?
   d) Is it socially responsive or transformative?
2) To 'do' your discipline to any sort of level, what do you need?
   a) Can you define the graduate attributes expected in terms of competencies?
   b) Are there particular attributes and traits that make for a successful practitioner?
   c) Do students understand the personal and emotional challenges involved in the discipline?
3) What verbs might describe what an accomplished person in your discipline can do?
   a) Using a full range of educational domains (cognitive, affective, psychomotor, metacognitive and inter-personal) – what verbs define the abilities of a successful graduate? [if you don't yet know what these are it will be covered later]
   b) Focus not on what student need to 'know', rather focus on what they need to be able to 'do'.
4) What should a degree at PG/UG level in your discipline involve? [Is there a Benchmark document?]
   a) What do students expect to engage in (fieldwork, project work, lab work, lectures, seminars, scenarios)
   b) What would be a meaningful rehearsal for work after graduation in your discipline?

We will reflect the answers to these questions in the Programme's aims and at programme level Intended Learning Outcomes. Once there is a consensus in the course design team as to the answers to these questions you can explore further.

Activity Four: Discipline Orientation

> Working with colleagues on a design team, it is worth spending some time exploring responses to the following four deceptively simple questions.
>
> If you don't find something to debate in response to these questions, you aren't trying hard enough!
>
> Asking yourself these simple questions, from both your own perspective as a practitioner and from a current student perspective. Even better use this as learning activity with your graduating students and ask them the same questions.
>
> It will undoubtedly produce some interesting conclusions.

Learning Orientations

The next filter we can use to create meaningful insight into who our potential students might be is to the POISE Epistemological model to consider our learners' orientation to study

This may come across as a more theoretical, or abstract notion, and may not suit your context. However, if you have a design or teaching team from different countries, speaking different mother tongues, and with varying educational experiences you will find this fascinating!

The POISE model is designed as an exploration of how the course team understands our students' potential orientation to learning.

By the time a student arrives at university to study, whether as an undergraduate or a postgraduate, their expectations of the discipline are not the only pre-formed attributes they possess. They also have a personal epistemology, or a concept of how knowledge is acquired, how they 'best' learn.

As a course team, it is sensible to spend some time trying to walk in your students' shoes and explore as much of their predispositions for learning, their personal epistemologies, as is possible. Again, the intention is not to stereotype groups of students, but to ensure that the learning you design is intended for them, not for you!

Here are five key themes that emerge for an analysis of the scholarship in this area (Atkinson, 2014). It is important that whilst there may be patterns in belief systems from individuals from the same cultural context, there will always be exceptions. Mapping your discipline expectations against these exceptions is a good place to start. Explore this table below, ask which of your potential students are likely to differ from your personal answers to these themes and associated questions. How do you think your students would react when confronted with the belief statements below.

Pneumonic	Binary concept	Tutorial Question	Belief statements
Pace	Quick or not at all	Is hard work enough?	Learning is quick or not all
Ownership	Authority or Reason	Who has the answers?	Knowledge is handed down by authority
Innateness	Innate or Acquired	Who is responsible for my learning?	The ability to learn is innate rather than acquired
Simplicity	Simple or Complex	Is there a simple answer?	Knowledge is simple rather than complex
Exactness	Certain or Tentative	Is there always a right answer?	Knowledge is certain rather than tentative

Table 2 - POISE Model

Ownership and Exactness are frequently cited as being culturally specific. There are cultural contexts in which the determination of the validity of knowledge is conferred in a particular social stratum (most often older men) and only these individuals have the authority to teach.

This contrasts with the dominant trait in European culture where knowledge is arrived at by reason. Therefore, the certainty of all knowledge in the European tradition is questionable. We often take it for granted that 'nothing is proven, simply yet to be disproved' is a universal concept; It isn't. Contemplating these personal epistemological dispositions of your students will help you design the learning process, particularly the orientation of each module, stage and programme.

There are some short animated videos that illustrate some reactions to POISE questions from international students in a British university context at https://sijen.com

How are your imaginary student profiles faring thus far?

Activity Five: Learning Orientations

This exercise can be challenging. Particularly if you encountered resistance to the early Student Inclusion Model 'game card'. At this point you may have members of your design team suggesting 'this is a waste of time'.

Bear with me. If you take the original personas that you generated in the card game, and ask them of each of the five POISE questions I guarantee the results will be of interest.

Make sure you annotate the whiteboard or slideshow, or however you recorded the Card Game results, with each of these new identifiers.

Personal Context

Now that we have tried to anticipate the dispositions of our students, we turn to more tangible evidence we might be able to access. In the colloquial sense we should be asking, "Where are my students coming from?"

Many of these questions will have been answered as you have developed responses to the educational and circumstantial dimensions, and you could interpret this exercise as validating your nascent student personas.

As a course team, you might draw up a list of more detailed questions based on the existing profile of students. But a good place to start would be to explore these five dimensions.

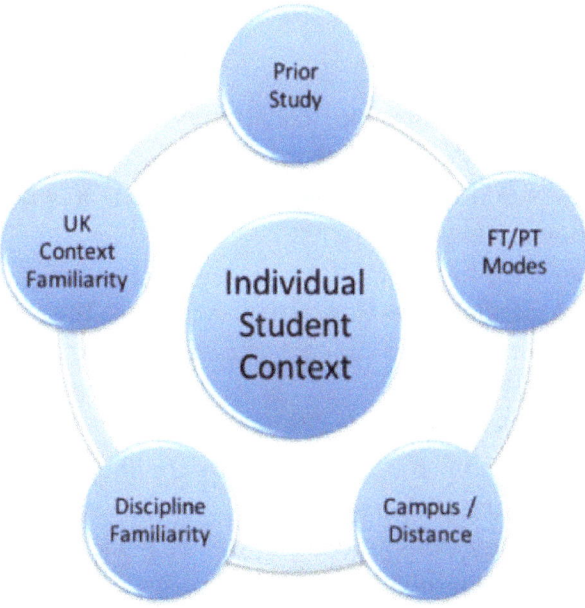

Figure 15 - Individual contexts

Answering them will prompt questions about preparedness for learning, media choice and learning support, all of which we go on in this framework to discuss.

Don't worry if you are left with lots of questions and few answers at this stage.

1) Prior Study
    a) Have your students already studied in the discipline, in the same context, and at an appropriate level?
    b) What patterns of learning will they be familiar with?
    c) What transitional learning arrangements make sense?
    d) How could the Accreditation of Prior Learning (APL) be identified?
2) FT/PT Mode
    a) What modes are you likely to deliver your programme or module in?
    b) Will students be familiar with the mode in which they are expected to learn?
    c) Will they have experienced the degree of independent learning anticipated, have they encountered the concept of blended learning before?
3) Campus/Distance
    a) What are students 'contextual experiences' prior to joining the University?
    b) Have they experienced campus-based learning, or distance learning?
    c) Students may have studied in very remote schools or been home schooled, all of which makes a

significant difference to their dispositions for learning.
4) Discipline Familiarity
   a) How much of the language of your discipline will be familiar to your students?
   b) How much of the fundamental concepts are required prior to joining the programme?
   c) How might you go about making sure that students have sufficient familiarity with the discipline prior to commencing study.
5) National (or Regional) Context Familiarity
   a) This is a tricky question, but it is useful to consider the degree to which students are already acculturated into the national or regional context.

Try not to get hung up on answering all these questions in a single workshop. It may be enough to share the questions and let them percolate through the design team's thought processes between design meetings.

Activity Six: Personal Context

By now you will begin to feel that you have a grasp on who these students are represented in your personas. You may even want to generate images to illustrate them.

You can use a site such as https://thispersondoesnotexist.com, or use any AI image generator and describe the person. It can just be helpful to start to solidify in your mind that students are human, most of them anyway.

Once you are happy that you have your four to eight personas, go through the questions form the personal context section and answer them for each of these individuals. You'll find it is getting a bit easier to guess or make assumptions, both of which are fine.

Social Context

Look again at your student profiles. Now, we can broaden our reflection to consider how such students might work as a cohort. You might want to adapt these questions to include further dimensions, but from a learning design perspective, I believe these are the most pertinent. It is not our concern to know about the private lives of our students, but understanding in general terms the 'nature' of the cohort (and being aware of its changing composition over time) can make learning design more meaningful.

Having created your student profiles, and answered the previous questions about personal contexts, it should now be clear how diverse or homogenous your cohorts are likely to be, and you can design learning for this. You could consider the following four thematic areas;

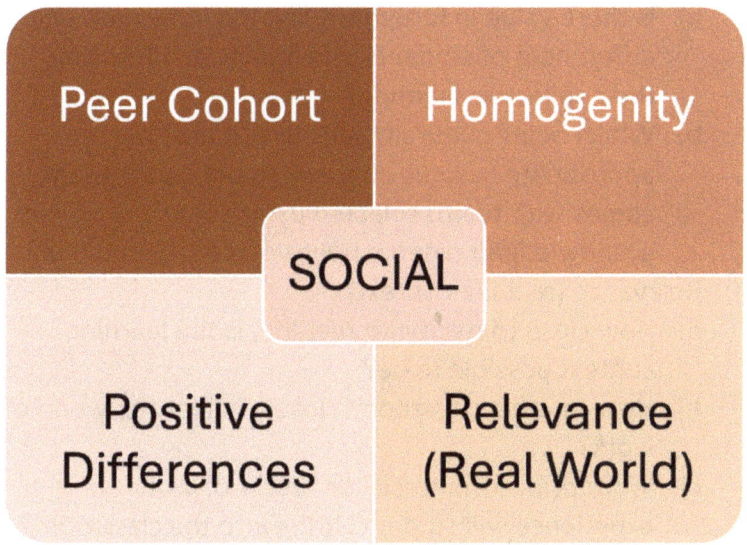

Figure 16 - Social Dimensions to Learning Cohorts

1) Peer Cohort
    a) Can you anticipate that it will be possible to leverage significant cohort learning, learning sets or teams for example?
    b) Will there be sufficient diversity in skills to warrant building mixed ability cohorts rather than allowing 'birds of a feather to flock together'?
2) Homogeneity
    a) If you anticipate a very similar profile to most students, how will you accommodate those that do not conform to the 'normal profile'?
    b) Is there sufficient challenge within a highly homogenous cohort?
3) Positive Difference
    a) Is there value in foregrounding the individual differences of students as a means of advancing their collective learning?
    b) Whilst being culturally sensitive, it may be appropriate in some contexts to anticipate team games with teams selected using some shared and acknowledged criteria. Have you considered this?
4) Relevance (real-life context)
    a) How close to reality, to real-life, is the learning context possible to be?
    b) How can the 'classroom' closely mirror the world of work?
    c) What prior commercial or 'world-of-work' experience will students bring into the classroom?

Activity Seven: Social Context

Go through the same process you carried out in Activity Six with the same four to eight personas.

Only now you are thinking about them as social animals rather than as isolated individuals. go through the questions form the personal co

This activity is important regardless of whether you anticipate students to be on-campus and in the same classrooms or studying remotely. Learning always happens in a social context. Always in their socio-cultural context, sometimes in the social construct you and your institution creates for them.

Working with your Personas

Your personas become touchstones for your designs. They are not immutable; they may change and adapt as you go through subsequent design stages.

An illustrative example

Here is a first-year undergraduate course taught at a British University. It is intended as an 'Introduction to Social Theory'. My design team is already discussing the merits of teaching through broad theoretical approaches or through the lens of specific thinkers, and whether this should be done chronologically.

By the time I have set myself up as the design workshop moderator, a heated argument has developed as to whether Augustine or Socrates is the best starting point.

Note to self: Academics generally have strong opinions!

Once rallied, I split the group into two teams of three. Each group consists of some colleagues who will teach different parts of the course, a couple of teaching assistants who may support this course and the senior academic who is Programme Director this course will sit in, namely a Bachelors in Sociology (BSc).

We begin with the 30-minute review of the history of the programme, its development, and its academic performance. We identify that the reason for the new course is two-fold. Firstly, because current foundation courses make what appear to be erroneous assumptions about the foundational learning students bring to this first year of their degree. Secondly, because this course is attracting a range of international students, notably from the United States of America but also from India, Malaysia and Thailand, where the university is actively marketing. These students come with little foundational learning.

> *Note to self: It is important not to get ahead of oneself.*

As the conversation begins to highlight individual perspectives on the school system in different countries and the 'quality' of recruits, I begin the first exercise.

First, we begin with each team thinking in broad terms about the assumptions that had been made in some of the current courses that make up the first year. We write up onto the board any emergent themes. These include language challenges for overseas students, lack of general knowledge (which translated to "why haven't they heard of Aristotle or Spinoza") and (more specifically) a lack of any foundation in western sociology or philosophy.

This was a critical reset moment. The entire design team realised that they had to put on the back-burner any notion of giving a broad overview of 'social theories', and rather would be required to unpack the relationship of social theories in their historical (and socio-political) context.

At one point, one of the participants made the observation:

> *How would you like to be taught about Chinese social theories if you were starting a degree in Sociology in China?*

A version of that question is always relevant. Regardless of the level and the discipline.

Having established just how "not like us", some of our students might be, as a design team we set about producing personas for eight possible, even probable, students. We followed both persona generating approaches starting with the Student Inclusion Model. We spent about two hours on this, both teams sharing ideas and reflections at various points.

A week later the design team came back together again. After a quick review of what had been concluded last time that I had written up since last we had all met, we then ran through the Four Quadrants exercises over the next three hours, allowing roughly 40 minutes for each

There was some heated debate as to whether the eight personas we had begun working with the previous week were turning into 'stereotypes', and this is always a danger. It is important for anyone working in this field to acknowledge their own socio-cultural lens. It is unavoidable, but it can be recognised and countered by others across a design team.

Remember your personas are not intended to be accurate descriptions of 'real' people. Quite the contrary, they are intended to be caricatures.

Evaluating Student Profiles

Each stage of the 8-Stage Learning Design Framework requires an evaluation process to be designed alongside and refined at the end of the process of design, to be used as part of an evaluation framework for active courses. Your institution may have an existing quality assurance mechanism in place, but if they don't here are a series of questions to get you started. Remember, these questions relate just to the effectiveness of your use of student profiles, not an evaluation of your whole course, each stage will generate evaluation questions which all come together in stage eight.

1. How homogenous have your cohorts been?
2. What has changed in terms of students' expectations, and how have you adjusted to these?
3. How have the personal profiles of students developed over the duration of previous, or the current courses or programmes?
4. What cultural differences have you detected and how have these been treated, as challenges or as opportunities?
5. How has the epistemological profile of your cohorts changed over time?
6. What impact is digitalisation having on your student profiles?
7. What impact might automation have on your student profiles?
8. What impact is globalisation having on your student profiles?
9. How has the discipline developed since the course was designed and how might it evolve over the next five or ten years?

Course Templates and Artificial Intelligence

Your institution may provide you with a course or program template within which you are expected to design. This is not necessarily a bad thing; it can gain you time to reflect more deeply on the nature of the design itself.

I do however believe that it lends to a more conservative approach to course creation, and it is harder to adapt and adopt new practices within an existing framework. As we already discussed there are certain prerequisites at an institutional level that are always going to constrain your course design. Stages two and three of the 8-stage learning design model will explore some of these restrictions in detail and suggest some ways of adapting to them if not circumventing them.

Where a course template is valuable is in the context of a programme design. Making sure that there is some consistency within the student experience across courses within a programme supports their learning. That does not mean that all the courses need to look the same, rather it means there is an alignment in terms of student effort, assessment types, and learning skills required.

One of the biggest complaints we often hear from our students is that their courses expected uneven amounts of work from them, often at the same time, and students were inevitably forced to prioritise between their courses.

Another complaint we often hear is that courses made assumptions as to the knowledge and skills that had already been acquired. Faculty teaching on a second-year course that have not bothered to check whether the skills they are assuming of their second-year student have been taught in that student's first year, for example.

Taking the time to run through all 8 stages of the eight-stage learning design framework when designing a new programme is the best place to start. If you are charged with designing a single course, or some portion of a year, then it is important to be able to articulate the shape of the wider programme and one means of doing that is to use the eight-stage learning design framework as a diagnostic instrument.

In this short guide we have explored the value of starting the process focusing on the students that are likely to enrol on your course or programme. More about the role of artificial intelligence will be discussed at later stages. Suffice it to say that the current tools that are readily available, ChatGPT being the most obvious, are not able to do the work for you in designing entire courses and programmes.

These AI tools, in their current form, cannot make the reflective and considered judgements that we have explored in the activities above. They cannot generate thoughtful and purposeful personas directly linked to your context.

These artificial intelligence tools can however be useful as part of the design process as almost a neutral colleague who has no real knowledge of your specific subject biases or those of your fellow design colleagues. Asking one of these AI tools for the key points around a specific subject for example, may throw up one or two that you had not already considered, or more likely serve simply as reassurance that you have covered all the key points. To treat these tools as sense-check instruments is where they are best serving designers currently in 2024.

There will undoubtedly be developments in this area provided by some of the commercial providers of the larger learning management systems. They are all most likely going to generate tools that can articulate a possible course outline and content, based on institutional histories. However, I would be extremely cautious of the validity of any of those designs given that they will have been trained on existing courses and programmes and risk simply perpetuating some of the existing fallacies that permeate higher education.

There is no substitute for taking a fresh approach to each course and programme design, and ensuring it is aligned to the needs of its future students. Those needs will include awareness of AI, and we will discuss that at stage three of the design process of the 8-SLDF.

Conclusion

I trust you will have this volume helpful as you consider who you are designing your programmes and courses for. I recognise that it is difficult, with time and resources limited, to find the time to design courses from their very foundations. It is so much easier to take an existing course and switch out the existing content with something new. It is often easier to get internal and external validation if your courses look familiar.

There is value I believe in spending a day, perhaps two, alone or with your design team considering who your students are going to be. This will allow you to reflect more effectively on the next two stages of the design framework, discipline and professional contexts and media choices. Ultimately it will produce a well-designed course.

The activities in this book are all optional. Indeed, I have rarely had the opportunity personally to carry out all these activities with a course design team. Variations on them, or even the time self-reflecting on each, is not time wasted. Good luck!

References

Anderson, L. W., & Krathwohl, D. R. (2001). *A taxonomy for learning, teaching, and assessing: A revision of Bloom's taxonomy of educational objectives.* Longman.

Atkinson, S. P. (2011a). Developing faculty to integrate innovative learning in their practice with the SOLE model. In S. Ferris (Ed.), *Teaching, Learning and the Net Generation: Concepts and Tools for Reaching Digital Learners.* IGI Global.

Atkinson, S. P. (2011b). Embodied and Embedded Theory in Practice: The Student-Owned Learning-Engagement (SOLE) Model. *The International Review of Research in Open and Distance Learning, 12*(2), 1–18.

Atkinson, S. P. (2014). *Rethinking personal tutoring systems: The need to build on a foundation of epistemological beliefs.* BPP University College.

Atkinson, S. P. (2015). Graduate Competencies, Employability and Educational Taxonomies: Critique of Intended Learning Outcomes. *Practice and Evidence of the Scholarship of Teaching and Learning in Higher Education, 10*(2), 154–177.

Atkinson, S. P. (2022). *Writing good learning outcomes and objectives: Short guide to creating well-structured intended learning outcomes that ensure effective course designs.* Sijen Education.

Bates, T. (2016). *The role of technology in distance education.* Routledge.

Biggs, J., & Collis, K. F. (1982). *Evaluating the Quality of Learning: Structure of the Observed Learning Outcome Taxonomy.* Academic Press Inc.

Biggs, J., & Tang, C. (2007). *Teaching for Quality Learning at University: What the Student does* (3rd ed.). Open University Press.

Bloom, B. S. (Ed.). (1956). *Taxonomy of Educational Objectives, Handbook 1: Cognitive Domain* (2nd edition). Addison-Wesley Longman Ltd.

Branch, R. M. (2009). *Instructional Design: The ADDIE Approach*. Springer US. https://doi.org/10.1007/978-0-387-09506-6

Burden, K., & Atkinson, S. P. (2009). Personalising teaching and learning with digital resources: DiAL-e Framework case studies. In J. O'Donoghue (Ed.), *Technology Supported Environment for Personalised Learning: Methods and Case Studies* (pp. 91–108). IGI Global.

Conole, G. (2014). The 7Cs of learning design: A new approach to rethinking design practice. In S. Bayne, C. Jones, M. de Laat, T. Ryberg, & C. Sinclair (Eds.), *Proceedings of the 9th International Conference on Networked Learning 2014* (pp. 502–509). Networked Learning Conference. http://www.networkedlearningconference.org.uk/abstracts/pdf/conole.pdf

Dalziel, J. (Ed.). (2016). *Learning design: Conceptualizing a framework for teaching and learning online*. Routledge is an imprint of the Taylor & Francis Group, an Informa Business.

Dave, R. H. (1967). *Psychomotor domain*. International Conference of Educational Testing, Berlin.

Gagné, R. M., Briggs, L. J., & Wager, W. W. (1992). *Principles of Instructional Design*. Harcourt Brace Jovanovich College Publishers.

Gagné, R. M., & Driscoll, M. P. (1988). *Essentials of learning for instruction* (2nd ed). Prentice Hall.

Krathwohl, D. R., Bloom, B. S., & Masia, B. B. (1956). *Taxonomy of Educational Objectives, Handbook II: Affective Domain*. David McKay Company, Inc.

Laurillard, D. (2002). *Rethinking University Teaching: A Conversational Framework for the Effective Use of Learning Technologies* (2nd ed). Routledge Falmer.

Laurillard, D. (2012). *Teaching as a Design Science* (1 edition). Routledge.

Lockwood, F. (Ed.). (1994). *Materials Production in Open and Distance Learning*. SAGE Publications Inc.

Merrill, M. D. (2013). *First principles of instruction: Assessing and designing effective, efficient, and engaging instruction* [Electronic resource]. Pfeiffer.

Rowntree, D. (1994). *Preparing Materials for Open, Distance and Flexible Learning: An Action Guide for Teachers and Trainers*. Routledge.

Sewell, A., Kennett, A., & Pugh, V. (2022). Universal Design for Learning as a theory of inclusive practice for use by educational psychologists. *Educational Psychology in Practice*, *38*(4), 364–378. https://doi.org/10.1080/02667363.2022.2111677

Thomas, L., & May, H. (2010). *Inclusive learning and teaching in higher education* (p. 72). Higher Education Academy. http://www.heacademy.ac.uk/system/files/inclusivelearningandteaching_finalreport.pdf

Young, C., & Perović, N. (2016). Rapid and Creative Course Design: As Easy as ABC? *Procedia - Social and Behavioral Sciences*, *228*, 390–395. https://doi.org/10.1016/j.sbspro.2016.07.058

A website supports this research, and other projects cited in this book. https://sijen.com

www.ingramcontent.com/pod-product-compliance
Lightning Source LLC
Chambersburg PA
CBHW061339040426
42444CB00011B/2996

www.ingramcontent.com/pod-product-compliance
Lightning Source LLC
Chambersburg PA
CBHW061341040426
42444CB00011B/3029